The Urbana Free Library

To renew: call 217-367-4057
or go to "*urbanafreelibrary.org*"
and select "Renew/Request Items"

PEST-SNIFFING DOGS

by Meish Goldish

Consultant: Christine Barsema
K-9 Detectives, LLC

New York, New York

Credits

Cover and Title Page, © AP Photo/Eric Risberg; Cover TR, © David Cooper/The Toronto Star/ZUMA Press/Newscom; Cover CR, © Rex Features via AP Images; Cover BR, © Stan Honda/AFP/Getty Images; TOC, © Rex Features via AP Images; 4, © John C. Abbott Nature Photography; 5, © Chad Batka/The New York Times/Redux; 6, © John C. Abbott Nature Photography; 7, © Chad Batka/The New York Times/Redux; 8, © Stan Honda/AFP/Getty Images; 9, © Masai/Shutterstock; 10, © Edwin Remsberg; 11L, © Dani Vernon Photography; 11R, © Jack Clark/Agstockusa/AGE Fotostock; 12L, © Nigel Cattlin/Visuals Unlimited/Corbis; 12R, © Bartomeu Borrell/AGE Fotostock/SuperStock; 13, © Jeff Roberson/KRT/Newscom; 14, © Matthew Roberts/NY Daily News; 15, © Ruby Washington/The New York Times/Redux; 16L, © Mike Pease/ZUMA Press/Newscom; 16R, © Stan Honda/AFP/Getty Images/Newscom; 17, © Joshua Sudock/The Orange County Register/ZUMA Press/Newscom; 18, © Mira Oberman/AFP/Getty Images/Newscom; 19, © AP Photo/Eric Risberg; 20, © David Cooper/The Toronto Star/ZUMA Press/Newscom; 21, © Mike Pease/ZUMA Press/Newscom; 22, © Rodger Richards/KRT/Newscom; 23T, © Chad Batka/The New York Times/Redux; 23B, © AP Photo/PRNewsFoto/Honig Vineyard; 24, © James Estrin/The New York Times/Redux; 25, © Brian Ray/SourceMedia Group News; 26, © William H. Mullins/Photo Researchers, Inc.; 27, © Rex Features via AP Images; 28, © Stan Honda/AFP/Getty Images/Newscom; 29TL, © Eric Isselée/Shutterstock; 29TR, © Jagodka/Shutterstock; 29BL, © Eric Isselée/Shutterstock; 29BR, © Eric Isselée/Shutterstock.

Publisher: Kenn Goin
Editorial Director: Adam Siegel
Creative Director: Spencer Brinker
Design: Dawn Beard Creative
Photo Researcher: Daniella Nilva

Library of Congress Cataloging-in-Publication Data

Goldish, Meish.
  Pest-sniffing dogs / by Meish Goldish.
    p. cm. — (Dog heroes)
  Includes bibliographical references and index.
  ISBN-13: 978-1-61772-454-1 (library binding)
  ISBN-10: 1-61772-454-8 (library binding)
  1. Detector dogs—Juvenile literature. 2. Search dogs—Juvenile literature. I. Title.
  SF428.2.G656 2012
  636.73—dc23

                    2011043248

For more information, write to Bearport Publishing Company, Inc., 45 West 21st Street, Suite 3B, New York, New York 10010. Printed in the United States of America in North Mankato, Minnesota.

10 9 8 7 6 5 4 3 2 1

Table of Contents

A Disturbing Find

One morning in 2010, a family in Brooklyn, New York, was preparing to move into a new house. Most of their belongings were already packed up in boxes. The mother was worried, however, because the night before, she had found a dead **bedbug** floating in a bathtub.

Bedbugs got their name because they often gather in beds to bite people when they are sleeping.

Bedbugs are hard to see. They are only about one-eighth to one-quarter inch (3.2 to 6.4 mm) long.

Were more of the tiny **pests** living in the family's home? To make sure the bedbugs didn't travel in any boxes or furniture to the new house, the parents called for a pest **inspector** to search for the **insects**—only the inspector who arrived wasn't a person. He was Cruiser, a dog!

Cruiser is a type of dog called a puggle— a cross between a pug and a beagle.

Bug Hunt

Cruiser began to inspect the home for bedbugs. First he carefully sniffed all the boxes that held the family's belongings. Within a few minutes, he **determined** that none of them contained any pests. Then the dog walked around to check out the furniture.

Bedbugs are often hard to find because they can crawl inside the tiny openings in furniture.

Bedbugs can hide in many items, including nightstands, carpets, clothing, furniture, luggage— even telephones and clocks!

Cruiser sniffed a wooden crib in one of the children's rooms. He pawed at the mattress. It was his way of saying, "I smell bedbugs here." The mother was upset but also grateful. Thanks to Cruiser, the insects could now be **exterminated**. They would not be moving with the family into their new home.

Cruiser smelled bedbugs hiding inside a mattress.

Dog Detectives

Cruiser is one of about 200 dogs in the United States that are trained to **detect** pests. Some dogs **specialize** in finding bedbugs. Other dogs are taught to sniff out different kinds of harmful insects, such as **termites** and **mealybugs**.

Freedom, a beagle, inspects a room for bedbugs.

Why are dogs used to hunt pests? For one thing, a **canine** is able to find bugs much more easily than a human can. Dogs can smell tiny bugs that are hard for people to see and impossible for them to smell. The dogs also work faster than humans. They can use their noses to inspect a room in minutes, while a person might take hours to look for the little pests. In addition, dogs can search in narrow spaces that people cannot reach.

According to a 2008 study at the University of Florida, pest-sniffing dogs are correct in their findings about 98 percent of the time.

A dog smells odors up to 100 times better than a person.

Pesky Pests

Pest-sniffing dogs do an important job. Without their help, harmful insects can spread and cause big problems. Bedbugs, for example, bite people to drink their blood. Although the insects are not dangerous and do not carry disease, their bites often leave ugly, itchy red marks on a victim's skin.

Bedbugs feed only on blood. They usually get it by biting people while they are sleeping, though they also attack birds and other animals.

Since the 1990s, California grape growers have battled a different kind of pest—**vine** mealybugs. These little insects attack farmers' **crops** by releasing a liquid from their bodies that causes grapes to turn **moldy**. Once damaged, the fruit cannot be sold or eaten. To stop the bugs from spreading, farmers sometimes use dogs to locate the tiny insects, which often hide on a plant's roots or under its bark. As a result of the dogs' detective work, the pests are often found and exterminated—and the grapes are saved.

A golden retriever sniffs for vine mealybugs.

A close-up view of a vine mealybug

Mealybugs can destroy many kinds of plants, including fruit trees, coffee trees, and sugarcane.

House Eaters

Another kind of pest that homeowners fear is termites. These antlike insects are dangerous because they eat wood. When thousands of termites gather together in a large **colony**, their wood-eating ways can destroy part or all of a house.

Termites eating wood

By eating wood, termites can weaken the **foundation** of a home and the boards that support the walls and roof.

In 2010, Ed Jenkins discovered termites in his home in North Carolina. He contacted exterminators, but they weren't able to figure out where the insects were entering the house. Luckily, two termite-hunting dogs, Silas and Jack, were brought in to solve the mystery. After sniffing around the property, the clever canines quickly discovered that the termites were tunneling into the house through the garage and a basement wall. The exterminators were then able to get rid of the pests for good.

This dog, like Silas and Jack, is trained to find termites.

Best for a Pest

Many dogs work as pest sniffers. Which **breeds** are best for the job? Surprisingly, no particular type is considered **superior**. Some bug hunters are beagles or Labrador retrievers, while others are terriers, spaniels, collies, or belong to one of many other breeds.

Radar, a bedbug hunter, is a beagle.

Many pest-sniffing dogs come from **shelters**. Often, the owners of these dogs gave them up because the canines were too energetic to be kept as pets. These kinds of dogs, however, are usually eager to perform some kind of job— which makes them perfect for pest sniffing!

Although people who train pest-sniffing dogs aren't concerned about the exact breed, they do look for certain qualities in the dogs they teach. The canines must be playful and full of energy. They also must be able to concentrate and not get easily **distracted**. In addition, some trainers prefer to work with smaller dogs, since the animals can squeeze into tight spaces when they are trying to sniff out pests.

Summer is a German shepherd that has been trained to find bedbugs.

School for Sniffing

Before a dog can hunt a pest, it must learn what the bug smells like. One place that teaches dogs to identify the **scents** of bugs is the Florida Canine Academy. It is run by Bill Whitstine. To train his dogs, he keeps live bedbugs in a **vial** covered with a piece of netting.

The bedbugs inside this vial are used to train pest-sniffing dogs.

Bill Whitstine taught this beagle to find termites.

The Florida Canine Academy is one of many schools in the United States that train pest-sniffing dogs. Training at most schools lasts about two to three months.

A dog begins its training by sniffing the bedbug scent coming from the vial. Each time the dog smells the bugs, it receives a treat. Soon, the dog is **conditioned** to want to find the odor. Later, vials are hidden in places such as inside boxes and under rugs. The dog must find the bugs to get a reward.

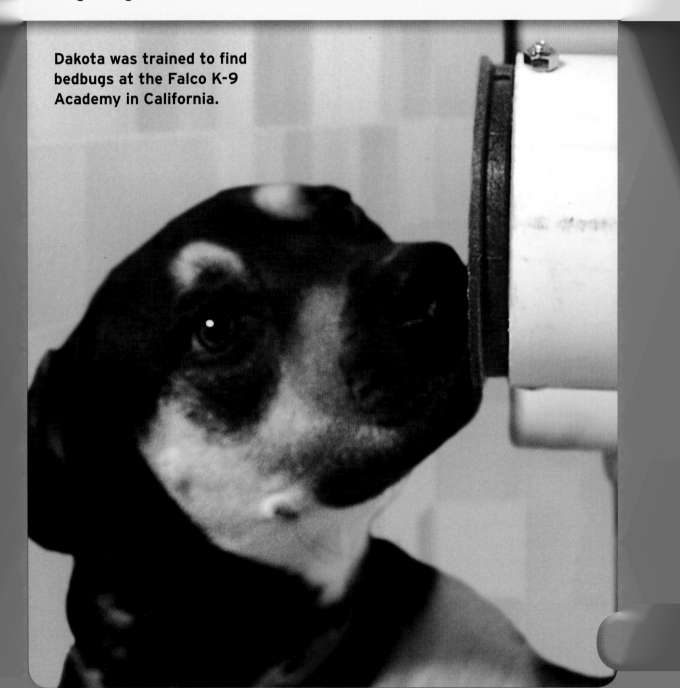

Dakota was trained to find bedbugs at the Falco K-9 Academy in California.

Staying on Target

Finding pest odors isn't as simple as it may sound. A bedbug sniffer, for example, must learn to detect only the scents of live bedbugs and their eggs. The dog must ignore the scents of related items, such as dead bedbugs from an earlier **infestation**. The dog must also ignore the odors of old bedbug eggshells and waste matter.

Bella sniffs different containers to find the one containing bedbugs.

During training, a dog sniffs many different vials. Some give off the odor the dog is being trained to find, while others give off odors to be ignored. The dog is rewarded only when it sniffs the correct odor.

A mealybug sniffer faces other challenges. Because mealybugs are often found outdoors on plants, shifting winds can cause a bug's odor suddenly to change direction. The dog, however, must be able to track the scent back to its source—the mealybug. The bug hunter also can't get distracted by rabbits or other animals running through the area that it is searching.

Nexus, a golden retriever, is hunting for vine mealybugs.

Smell and Tell

Once a dog sniffs the odor it is searching for, the clever canine must let the trainer know that it has found the scent. Some trainers teach their dogs to signal by touching the item that the scent is coming from with their paws. Other trainers don't like to use that method. They fear the dog may accidentally scratch the furniture or spread the bugs around. As a result, some dogs are trained to signal in other ways.

This dog uses its paw to signal that it has found bedbugs.

Gracie, a Cavalier King Charles spaniel, is a graduate of the Florida Canine Academy. She was taught to signal that she had found a scent by sitting quietly, pointing her nose in the direction of her discovery, and looking up at her handler. When she found the correct odor, she was rewarded with a treat.

Some trainers teach their dogs to bark in the direction of the bug scent they have found.

This beagle looks up at his trainer to show that he has found a container with termites in it.

Work Partners

After a dog has been trained to sniff for pests, it is sold to a **handler**. That's the person who will work with the canine on the job. Before receiving a dog, however, the handler must go through a week of training. He or she is taught how to treat the animal both at work and at home.

A termite-sniffing Jack Russell terrier named Tracker snuggles with her handler, Kevin Kordek.

TRACKER

A pest-sniffing dog lives with its handler, who cares for the animal and plays with it when the two are not working together.

Being able to tell whether a dog is giving a signal to show that it has found something is one of the most important things a handler needs to learn. If the handler is unsure, he or she should give the dog another opportunity to search the area. The handler also needs to learn how to use the scent vials to retrain the dog on a daily basis. That way, the canine never forgets the odor it is looking for.

Some bedbug handlers feed the pests they use to retrain their dogs. The handlers let the bugs bite their arms to give them the blood they need to live.

A handler must learn not to lead the dog in any particular direction as it hunts for bugs. Instead, the canine should be allowed to search freely on its own.

On the Job

Carl Massicott is a busy handler. He runs Advanced K9 Detectives, a company with many pest-sniffing dogs. All of them specialize in finding bedbugs. Each dog can work up to eight hours a day. The handler usually gives the animal a 15- or 20-minute break every hour, to keep it from getting tired.

Massicott's dog Jada checks out a room for bedbugs.

Massicott's dogs are always on the go. In New York City alone, the number of reported bedbug cases rose from 537 in 2004 to nearly 13,000 in 2010. As a result, the canine detectives are kept busy, sniffing out bugs in houses, apartments, nursing homes, offices, hotels, stores, movie theaters—even cruise ships. "It's difficult to keep up with the demand," Massicott said.

Jackson, a Jack Russell terrier, searches a room for bedbugs in the Hawkeye Motel in Iowa.

Many pest-inspection companies charge about $300 an hour to have their dogs sniff out a house or building.

Past, Present, and Future

The problem of pests is nothing new. Bedbugs, for example, were a **nuisance** in America as early as the 1800s. By the 1960s, however, a powerful chemical called DDT was used to kill bedbugs and many other insects. The poison helped stop bedbugs from spreading. Yet in 1972 the U.S. government **banned** DDT. Scientists had discovered that it harmed or killed many plants and animals that lived near the areas where DDT was sprayed.

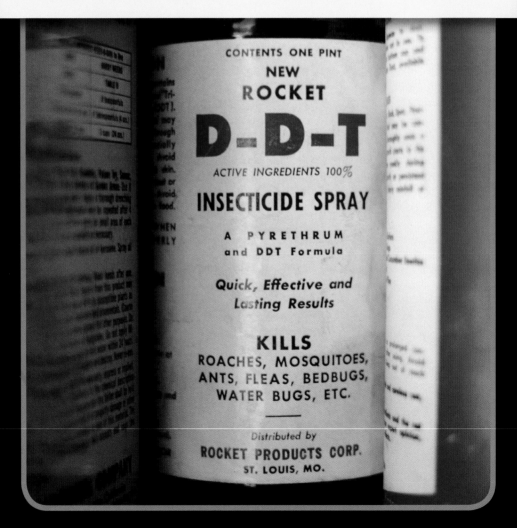

CONTENTS ONE PINT
NEW
ROCKET

D-D-T

ACTIVE INGREDIENTS 100%

INSECTICIDE SPRAY

A PYRETHRUM
and DDT Formula

*Quick, Effective and
Lasting Results*

KILLS
ROACHES, MOSQUITOES,
ANTS, FLEAS, BEDBUGS,
WATER BUGS, ETC.

Distributed by
ROCKET PRODUCTS CORP.
ST. LOUIS, MO.

DDT was banned after scientists discovered that it also poisoned many other living things besides pests.

Today, many scientists believe that the ban on DDT may explain why bedbugs have now returned to the United States in record numbers. Another reason for their increase may be that many people are now traveling to parts of the world where bedbugs are more common—and some of the pests are returning to the United States hidden in suitcases. Exterminators are trying to battle the pests with less harmful chemicals as well as other methods. For the present, however, the best weapon for finding the bugs continues to be well-trained pest-sniffing dogs.

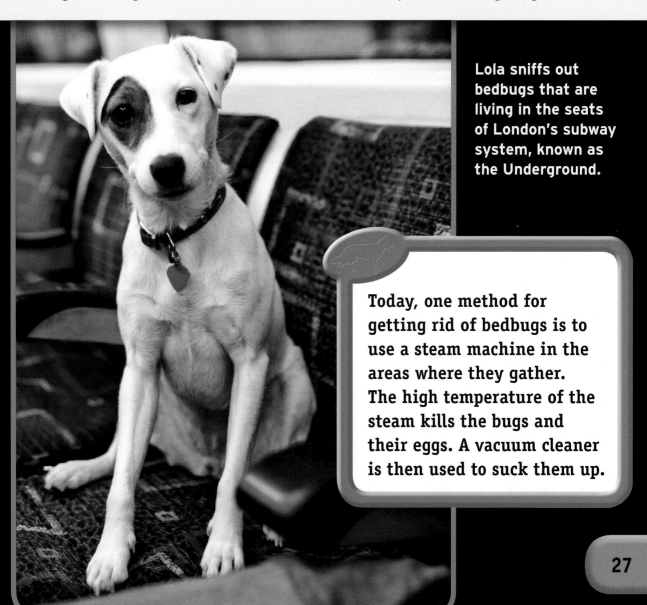

Lola sniffs out bedbugs that are living in the seats of London's subway system, known as the Underground.

Today, one method for getting rid of bedbugs is to use a steam machine in the areas where they gather. The high temperature of the steam kills the bugs and their eggs. A vacuum cleaner is then used to suck them up.

Just the Facts

- A dog has about 220 million **cells** in its nose for smelling, while a person has only about 5 million cells for smelling.

- A bedbug-sniffing dog can check out an average-size hotel room in less than two minutes.

- When people hunt for termites hidden inside the walls of a home, they usually find them about 30 percent of the time. Pest-sniffing dogs can find the insects more than 90 percent of the time.

- Pest-sniffing dogs may miss an odor if it is coming from a bug that is too high above their heads. For example, dogs may not detect insects that are on a ceiling. However, some pest-sniffing dogs have been known to find bedbugs hiding high above them in light fixtures!

Freedom searches for bedbugs in a home in Queens, New York.

Common Breeds: PEST-SNIFFING DOGS

Labrador retriever

golden retriever

German shepherd

beagle

banned (BAND) ordered something not to be used or done

bedbug (BED-bug) a bloodsucking insect sometimes found in beds

breeds (BREEDZ) kinds of dogs

canine (KAY-nine) a member of the dog family

cells (SELZ) basic, very tiny parts of a person, animal, or plant

colony (KOL-uh-nee) a large group of insects that live together

conditioned (kuhn-DISH-uhnd) trained to behave a certain way

crops (KROPS) plants grown in large amounts, usually for food

detect (di-TEKT) to notice or discover something

determined (di-TUR-mind) discovered; found out

distracted (dis-TRAKT-id) having one's attention drawn away by something

exterminated (ek-STUR-muh-*nayt*-id) killed in large numbers

foundation (foun-DAY-shuhn) a solid structure on which a building is built

handler (HAND-lur) a person who trains and works with an animal that does a job

infestation (in-fess-TAY-shuhn) a condition of being filled with harmful insects

insects (IN-sekts) small animals that have six legs, three main body parts, two antennas, and a hard covering called an exoskeleton

inspector (in-SPEK-tur) someone who checks or examines things

mealybugs (MEEL-ee-*bugz*) insects that attack and destroy plants

moldy (MOHLD-ee) covered with a woolly or furry growth, called a fungus, that causes decay

nuisance (NOO-suhnss) something that is annoying and causes problems

pests (PESTS) animals, such as insects, mice, or spiders, that bother or annoy people

scents (SENTS) smells or odors

shelters (SHEL-turz) places where homeless animals can stay

specialize (SPESH-uh-*lize*) to focus on one area of work

superior (suh-PIHR-ee-ur) above average in quality or ability

termites (TUR-mites) antlike insects that eat wood

vial (VYE-uhl) a small, thin glass or plastic bottle

vine (VINE) a plant with a long stem that grows along the ground or climbs by attaching itself to trees, fences, or walls

Bibliography

Eisenberg, Jeff. *The Bed Bug Survival Guide: The Only Book You Need to Eliminate or Avoid This Pest Now.* New York: Grand Central Publishing (2011).

Godfrey, Kris E., Kent M. Daane, Walt J. Bentley, Raymond J. Gill, and Raksha Malakar-Kuenen. *Mealybugs in California Vineyards.* Oakland, CA: University of California (2002).

Kaldenbach, Jan. *K9 Scent Detection.* Calgary, Canada: Detselig Enterprises (1998).

Syrotuck, William G. *Scent and the Scenting Dog.* Mechanicsburg, PA: Barkleigh Productions (2000).

Read More

Aloian, Molly, and Bobbie Kalman. *Helpful and Harmful Insects.* New York: Crabtree (2005).

Bueche, Shelley. *Bedbugs.* Detroit, MI: KidHaven (2005).

Goldish, Meish. *Bomb-Sniffing Dogs (Dog Heroes).* New York: Bearport (2012).

Markle, Sandra. *Termites: Hardworking Insect Families.* Minneapolis, MN: Lerner (2008).

Stamper, Judith Bauer. *Eco Dogs (Dog Heroes).* New York: Bearport (2011).

Learn More Online

Visit these Web sites to learn more about the insects that pest-sniffing dogs find:

http://kidshealth.org/kid/ill_injure/bugs/bedbug.html

www.biokids.umich.edu/critters/Isoptera/

www.pestworldforkids.org/bedbugs.html

www.pestworldforkids.org/termites.html

Index

About the Author

Meish Goldish has written more than 200 books for children.
His book *Heart-Stopping Roller Coasters* was a Children's Choices
Selection in 2011. He lives in Brooklyn, New York.